State of the Union

THE INTERGOVERNMENTAL CONFERENCE OF THE EUROPEAN UNION 1996

Federal Trust Paper Number One

Federal Trust Round Table

In December 1994 the Federal Trust established a Round Table to discuss in depth the issues raised by the 1996 Intergovernmental Conference of the European Union, to monitor the processes of its preparation, negotiation and ratification, and to assess its outcome. A series of *Federal Trust Papers* will be published. The Round Table is chaired by Lord Jenkins of Hillhead, President of the European Commission 1977-81; the rapporteur is John Pinder, Chairman of the Federal Trust; the secretary is Andrew Duff, Director of the Trust, to whom any written comments should be addressed.

Members of the Round Table serve in an independent capacity and do not represent their organisations. They do not necessarily concur with all the opinions expressed in this *Federal Trust Paper*, but they support its general thrust and welcome it as a contribution to the debate about the future of the Union.

The Federal Trust is an independent charity and, as such, holds no political view of its own.

The Round Table includes:

Lord Lester QC
Jean-Victor Louis
Sarah Ludford
Peter Luff
David Marquand
Andrew Marr
David Martin MEP
Richard Mayne
David Millar
Gary Miller
Frances Morrell
Edward Mortimer
Sir William Nicoll
Simon Nuttall
Sir Michael Palliser
Robin Pedler
John Pinder
Roy Pryce
Giles Radice MP
Paul Richards
Keith Richardson
Francesco Rossolillo

Malcolm Rutherford
Derek Scott
Michael Shackleton
Eleanor Sharpston
John Stevens MEP
Susan Strange
Alastair Sutton
Susie Symes
Dick Taverne QC
Christopher Taylor
Anthony Teasdale
Lord Tugendhat
Sandy Walkington
Helen Wallace
William Wallace
Graham Watson MEP
Wolfgang Wessels
Shirley Williams
John Williamson
Ernest Wistrich
Stephen Woodard

Glossary

CAP	Common Agricultural Policy
CDU	Christian Democratic Union
CIS	Commonwealth of Independent States
CSCE	Conference on Security and Cooperation in Europe
CSU	Christian Social Union
EC	European Community
Ecu	European Currency Unit
EEA	European Economic Area
EMU	Economic and Monetary Union
ERM	Exchange Rate Mechanism
EU	European Union
Gatt	General Agreement on Tariffs and Trade
IGC	Intergovernmental Conference
NACC	North Atlantic Cooperation Council
Nato	North Atlantic Treaty Organisation
PFP	Partnership for Peace
OECD	Organisation for Economic Cooperation & Development
OSCE	Organisation for Security and Cooperation in Europe
WEU	Western European Union

Foreword by
Rt Hon Lord Jenkins of Hillhead

Europe has become immensely complicated. It has also become obfuscated by an unbalanced argument. The imbalance results from two factors. First, the pro-European case has recently been allowed to go by default. This arises from the defensive ambiguity of the government and partly from an apparent loss of nerve, for which I blame myself at least as much as others, on the part of the outside pro-Europeans. The second factor is largely made up of the drip, drip, drip of blaming Brussels for every ill, real and imaginary, that man (and woman) are heir to, while the positive case involves raising much wider considerations of history, geopolitics, security, world economic trends and the long-term outlook for Britain, all of which are at a discount in the low level of current political debate.

A large, experienced and quite wide-ranging group (the Round Table) has therefore come together under the aegis of the Federal Trust to try, in the approach to the Intergovernmental Conference of 1996, both to introduce some clarity into the complications and to redress the imbalance. All of these participating are broadly 'pro-European', but they span different political parties, and in spite of the name of the initiating body, would not all describe themselves as 'federalists', whatever meaning that somewhat abused word now has in popular consciousness. Nor do they seek utopian solutions. It is for instance stated bluntly in the paper that 'outside the field of defence, no new field of competence needs to be transferred from member states' governments to the (European) Union institutions'. What we rather seek is a constructive programme which, with only a little leap of the imagination, a British government might put forward at the IGC.

This does, however, involve facing up to some inescapable choices. Two aims of British policy command a wide measure of support: further enlargement, particularly to the East, and reform of the Common Agricultural Policy. Some however wish a third objective, which is the right of every member state to be able to say 'no' on any issue it chooses. Yet a Union of 20, 25, maybe even 30 states with a *liberum veto* would be a paralysed Union; and the CAP will never be reformed except on the basis of a majority, not an unanimous vote. And without CAP reform enlargement to the old Iron Curtain countries will be impossible from a budgetary point of view. So a failure to face issues leads not to muddling through but to the whole enterprise falling apart, which can only be welcomed by those who want frustrated chaos in Europe.

Another clear note struck in the Paper is that Europe needs more democracy. The Union is founded upon a democratic qualification. Only states which fulfil it are eligible for membership. And the fact of membership has undoubtedly helped to underpin democracy where it has been shaky in Spain, in Portugal, in Greece, and maybe now in Italy too. Yet the Union's own institutions, Council of ministers, Parliament and Commission have democratic deficits, for the correction of which there is obvious need and scope.

This paper is the general introduction to a series which the Round Table intends to publish over the next year or so. The next two will deal respectively with the institutions of Europe and with monetary union. We hope that they will clarify the debate and engage with the realities of the options open to Britain.

Roy Jenkins

January 1995

What Europe needs from 1996

A success story

Over the years, the European Union has brought the great benefits of peace and prosperity to its member states and citizens. It has restored democratic values in Europe. It has built a customs union and single market, negotiated major reductions in barriers to world trade and established important aid and development agreements with the world's poorest countries. Moreover, the Union has weathered a most serious economic recession.

The Union's rules and institutions have pioneered a new form of relations that preserves national identities while building ever closer union. It represents a partnership between states that is based on a rule of law directly applicable to the individual citizen of each state as well as equally to the states themselves, both large and small. And it has enlarged from the original six to fifteen member states, with a population of 370 million.

A time for action

The European Union has now reached a crucial stage in its development. The prospect of economic and monetary union, planned by the Treaty of Maastricht, is not far off. And the anxieties and aspirations of Central and Eastern Europe, liberated from communism, give the Union important new challenges and opportunities.

An Intergovernmental Conference to reform the European Union will begin in 1996. It should:

- ◆ make the Union more democratic;
- ◆ make the Union more efficient;
- ◆ build public confidence in the Union;
- ◆ prepare the Union for enlargement to the East.

Unfinished business

The Treaty of Maastricht left much unfinished business. The single market programme must be completed. Fraud must be checked. Our competitiveness worldwide and employment problems at home have to be tackled. Much practical work remains to be done if the single currency is to be introduced. The foundations for the information society in Europe need to be laid.

Preparations have to be made within both the applicant countries and the European Union for future enlargement. The Union must increase its effectiveness in foreign policy; it needs to incorporate WEU and to marry its security capability with that of Nato. It should also press forward its reform of the common agricultural policy. The potential member states have to deepen their economic and social development. Liberal democracy needs reinforcement everywhere.

Clear pacts, long friendships

Enlargement to the East may change the Union so much that agreement on core values and political goals must precede it. Citizens of the European Union need to know how they are governed, by whom and from where. They also need to be encouraged to participate. *Patti chiari, amicizia lunga.*

The Intergovernmental Conference must work to simplify and clarify the constitution of the Union. Outside the field of defence, no new field of competence needs to be transferred from member states' governments to the Union institutions. But while the scale of common government at the European level should remain modest, its profile should be more clearly visible.

The power and effectiveness of the European Parliament must be increased; the Commission must become more accountable, and the Council more open and democratic. In the law-making process of the Union the European Parliament, which represents the citizen-elector, should be elevated to share power with the Council, which represents the member states.

Such reforms will reinforce the federal element in the make up of the European Union. We recognise that in the United Kingdom the term 'federal' has acquired a specific meaning of its own unknown elsewhere. In mainland Europe, as indeed generally, federalism means that powers are shared and coordinated between the various levels of government — European, national and local — according to the rule of law and the principle of subsidiarity. It is in this sense that we use the term.

Dilemma for Britain

The United Kingdom has stressed its desire to be at the heart of Europe. It can remain there only if it makes constructive proposals to increase the Union's efficiency and democracy. The UK has the power to destabilise the Union or to add its weight to the building of a genuine European democracy.

The Union needs to have at its centre a core of governments committed to European integration. In case the UK or any other member state is tempted to veto the strengthening of the Union, the Intergovernmental Conference of 1996 should revise the Treaty to enable such a core to develop.

Here we set the scene for the Intergovernmental Conference. In subsequent *Federal Trust Papers* we will look at the European Union in detail and make further recommendations.

State of the Union [1]

'*Let us try to see how a Europe of around thirty members can function ...*' JACQUES DELORS, Les Echos, 6 December 1994

'*My strong suspicion is that we will see very little change of any serious nature, certainly no serious constitutional change.*' JOHN MAJOR, Financial Times, 20 December 1994

The Maastricht bequest

Sometime in 1996 there will begin an Intergovernmental Conference of the European Union (EU). Its official purpose is to revise the Treaties 'with the aim of ensuring the effectiveness of the mechanisms and the institutions of the Community'.[2]

The European Community dates back to 1951, and its aims were to build peace, unity and prosperity between its six founding member states. Membership of the EC involved the pooling of traditional national sovereignty and a commitment not just to international cooperation but also to economic and political integration — in other words, the establishment in limited fields of elements of common government. The bold experiment has been successful, notably with the foundation of the customs union and then the single market for goods, services, capital and people, and now the programme for economic and monetary union. To continue that success, however, and to adapt its institutions for the twenty-first century, it is widely accepted that there now has to be further political reform of the Community and the new 'Union' which was created by the Treaty of Maastricht in 1993.

The need for reform is urgent because membership of the EU, already grown to fifteen members, is seen to be a durable and attractive proposition for many other European countries. This is particularly so for those in Central Europe so recently liberated from communist dictatorships.

All who wish Europe well must realise that the Union's further enlargement will lead to its disintegration unless its institutions are modernised and made more efficient and democratic. Everyone agrees it is important to enhance the Union's image and credibility. But there is much disagreement about precisely what to do.

The Treaty of Maastricht, which sets up the Intergovernmental Conference (IGC) for 1996, bequeaths some tricky problems of unfinished business as well as itself complicating further the decision-making processes of the Union.

The issues prescribed for the 1996 IGC by the Treaty of Maastricht are as follows:

- to consider a report on the future security and defence arrangements of the Union, including the future of Western European Union (WEU);[3]
- to reappraise the 'three pillar' structure of the Union;[4]
- to consider widening the scope of the co-decision procedure;[5]
- to revisit the question of the classification by hierarchy of Community legislative acts;[6]
- to consider the introduction to the Treaty of specific clauses in the fields of civil protection, energy and tourism.[7]

All but the last injunction are in themselves of great constitutional significance, especially those which strengthen the powers of the European Parliament.

The whole question of the future security and defence arrangement of the Union, where swift progress has to be made in order to stabilise the Atlantic Alliance, is urgent and inescapable. In addition, since Maastricht was signed, the big controversy over voting in the Council — effectively the question of states' rights vis-à-vis the Union and the balance between large and small states — has been added to the IGC's agenda; and as part of the accession agreement with the new member states, it was also agreed that the IGC would return to the question of the size of the Commission.[8]

The Group of Reflection

The IGC will be prepared by a 'Group of Reflection' which was set up by the European Council at Corfu in June 1994 and requested to begin its work in June 1995, once the French presidential elections are well out of the way. This Group will consist of representatives of the fifteen governments, the European Commission and the European Parliament.[9]

The Group of Reflection was given a comprehensive mandate by the Corfu European Council to consider not only those items laid down by Maastricht but also 'any other measure deemed necessary to facilitate the work of the institutions and guarantee their effective operation in the perspective of enlargement'.[10] It will not have an easy task.

The challenges facing Europe are well-known and self-evidently serious: on the economic front, unemployment, a polluted environment and lack of competitiveness; in strategic terms, military insecurity and political instability in Central and Eastern Europe and the Mediterranean; within society, racism, poverty, poor education and training; and in politics, a fracturing of the nation state and its institutions, with a democratic deficit in the Union itself. The European Union is neither responsible for, nor will it resolve, all these problems. But it could take a lead by tackling at least some of them; and its Intergovernmental Conference is the next and best opportunity to do so. This first *Federal Trust Paper* examines the state of the European Union at the outset of this process, and discusses some of the options before the Group of Reflection.

Clearly the IGC will not be the only pressing item of business on the Union's agenda in 1996. The institutions will have to continue to bring fully into force the Treaty of Maastricht, not least the transition to Stage Three of Economic and Monetary Union (EMU), at the same time as they seek to improve upon it. They will also have to complete the task of implementing the decisions that flow from the White Paper of the Delors Commission *Growth, Competitiveness and Employment*.[11] Europe is emerging from economic recession, but the perennial debate about further steps to liberalise the still-incomplete European single market will be heavily focused on

3

several key sectors of the European economy, such as aviation, pensions, insurance, computers and telecommunications.[12] [SEE TABLE ONE] Austria, Finland and Sweden, the three new member states, will still be in the process of adaptation. The countries of Central Europe will be at the gates waiting for their entry with increasing impatience; and this requires, among other things, radical reform of the common agricultural policy and structural funds. Beyond them, Bosnia and other problems in Eastern Europe and the CIS will continue to confront the Common Foreign and Security Policy. Maintaining a working partnership with the United States will remain a major concern.

TABLE ONE

THE EU's GDP GROWTH					
Percentage change					
1991	1992	1993	1994	1995	1996
+ 1.5	+ 1.1	- 0.4	+ 2.6	+ 2.9	+ 3.2

Source: European Commission

It is also worth recalling that this IGC will begin while memories of the problematical Maastricht process are still fresh in the collective mind of the institutions, and while several of the main players (notably, Chancellor Kohl) are still in office. We should not forget that the Maastricht experience was a big shock to those responsible for the conduct of the Community. Democratic forces almost rejected the project, and caused leaders to stare rejection in the face. Happily, this *vertige identitaire* has sharpened the debate about the democratic legitimacy of the Union. There is now much more willingness among many of the governments to make the Community more 'user-friendly', to simplify procedures and clarify competences, and to confront some of the institutional implications of further enlargement.

Alternative futures

So how should we prepare to judge the IGC? The Conference will succeed in one sense if it reaches agreement on rectifying the technical problems that impede the smooth running of the inter-institutional procedures. There are some, like the British Prime Minister, who adopt this minimalist approach. But we believe that to resist more radical, structural reform of the Union at this stage would serve to increase public disillusion in Europe. If the European Union fails to become more efficient and democratic the quality of policy emerging, somewhat elliptically, from 'Brussels' will deteriorate and it will become more and more evident that the Union is failing to deal with our common problems. There is clearly a danger in these circumstances that popular consent to continued European integration will be withdrawn, and that the Union will then founder.[13]

The consequences of European disintegration could well be frightful, and would, to say the least, impoverish the quality of life in Europe while negating Europe's influence in world affairs. Of course, most of those who would resist deeper European integration, and are content with intergovernmental cooperation, would not welcome disintegration. But we believe that a shallow Europe would be unable to avoid disunity and eventual conflict in which national sovereignty preciously preserved would be practically useless.

There are those, for example in Britain, who seem to welcome such a scenario. They believe that the sovereignty of the British nation state must remain indivisible and inviolate. They hold to the notion that sovereignty resides uniquely in Parliament at Westminster, and would prefer to keep Britain well out of continental entanglements that require it to be shared.

There are others, however, who wish within Britain to temper traditional parliamentary sovereignty with the exercise of a modern popular sovereignty, and who seek new ways to articulate the aspirations and apprehensions of Britain's diverse peoples and communities: to reform Parliament, to decentralise government from Whitehall and Westminster, and to enhance the rights of British citizens. For us, too, it is logical to share power with our partners in common institutions in the European dimension. We see no bright future for the British people unless they engage fully in the economics, culture and politics of Europe. Accordingly, we want the UK government to play a full part in all aspects of European integration and to accept that there will be implications for the way we conduct our own affairs at home.

In short, we welcome the fact that Britain, having lost her Empire, can now find a new role in Europe. Our ambition for the European Union is that it should play a leading part in world affairs. We believe that the Union offers the hope of stability and security to the whole of Europe. That is why we supported the main thrust of the Union's development in the Treaty of Maastricht.[14] For us, the IGC in 1996 takes place at a time when definitive choices about Europe's alternative futures could and should be taken. It is indeed our firm view that the IGC must take important steps to enable the EU to fulfil its historic objectives of peace, unity and prosperity.

There is a serious danger that the IGC will fail. There seems to be a growing divergence of opinion about the future of a European Union that is itself growing in diversity. Common interests are being obscured by partisan and nationalist argument. For the IGC to succeed, politicians must devalue the cult of indivisible national sovereignty and, in its place, elevate the sharing of sovereignty in a united Europe. It is axiomatic to us that through unity and peace come prosperity and social justice. But without radical political and institutional change within the Union, European unification will not be assured. Then the Union would have failed Europe, and Europe would have failed the world.

The dynamics of Treaty revision

Like the Single Act before it, the Treaty on European Union, which came into force on 1 November 1993, included a revision clause.[15] The drafting of the Treaty had been marked by controversy, even rancour; and the undertaking to set up a review reflected both the determination of some member states to seek redress for specific grievances as well as a general apprehension that all which flowed from Maastricht would be far from perfect and that much unfinished business had been left behind. What the future held for the new Union, however, was not clearly forseen and no consensus formed among member governments about what was in store. The difficult process of ratifying the Treaty in many member states had evinced several different interpretations of what was contained within it; and the ratification in some member states — notably Denmark, France, Germany and the UK — had been revisionist in character.

Article N of Maastricht, therefore, is a significant one. It says that a conference of representatives of the governments of member states shall be convened in 1996 to examine those provisions of the Treaty for which revision is provided, in accordance with the aims of the Union. It is worthwhile recalling what those goals are.[16]

The Treaty of Maastricht was held to mark a new stage in the process of creating an ever closer union among the peoples of Europe.[17] The task of the new European Union is 'to organise, in a manner demonstrating consistency and solidarity, relations between the member states and between their peoples'. The first objective of the Union is to promote balanced and sustainable economic and social progress respectful of the environment, based on a single market and a single currency. The second objective is to assert its international identity through a common foreign and security policy, 'which might in time lead to a common defence'. The third is to strengthen European citizenship. The fourth is to develop close cooperation on justice and home affairs. And the fifth is to build on the *acquis communautaire* by revising the Treaty.[18] Explicitly, the Intergovernmental Conference of 1996 is to consider 'to what extent the policies and forms of cooperation introduced by this Treaty may need to be revised with the aim of ensuring the effectiveness of the mechanisms and the institutions of the Community'.[19] All this must be achieved while respecting the federalist principle of subsidiarity.

Subsidiarity: a two-edged sword

Subsidiarity is the rule that guides decisions about what action should be carried out at which level of government. Applied properly, subsidiarity seeks to guard against both the over-centralisation of government and its exaggerated dispersal. Under the Treaties establishing the European Communities (and now Union), competence over different areas of policy is either transferred exclusively to the Community level or shared between the EC institutions and member states or kept exclusively within the jurisdiction of the member state. This power-sharing exercise is neither very simple nor totally clear. Allegedly at the insistence of the Germans, subsidiarity was made explicit in the Treaty of Maastricht in order to overcome this ambiguity. Although we will try to avoid quoting many Treaty clauses, it is certainly worth citing in full the

7

Treaty's attempt to define subsidiarity because it goes to the heart of the debate about the future of the Union. Article 3b says:

> 'The Community shall act within the limits of the powers conferred upon it by this Treaty and of the objectives assigned to it therein.
>
> 'In areas which do not fall within its exclusive competence, the Community shall take action, in accordance with the principle of subsidiarity, only if and in so far as the objectives of the proposed action cannot be sufficiently achieved by the Member States and can therefore, by reason of the scale or effects of the proposed action, be better achieved by the Community.
>
> 'Any action by the Community shall not go beyond what is necessary to achieve the objectives of this Treaty'.

Elsewhere, the Treaty complicates matters.[20] In one place it says that decisions of the Union should be taken 'as closely as possible to the citizen'.[21] In another it says that the Union shall 'provide itself with the means necessary to attain its objectives and carry through its policies'.[22] And the Treaty of Maastricht left untouched the very important Article 235 of the EC Treaty, which says:

> 'If action by the Community should prove necessary to attain, in the course of the operation of the common market, one of the objectives of the Community and this Treaty has not provided the necessary powers, the Council shall, acting unanimously on a proposal from the Commission and after consulting the European Parliament, take the appropriate measures'.

It is necessary to note that Article 235, although permissive, is not a power of general competence. Article 235 can now only be used in accordance with Article 3b. The Community cannot do anything it wants. It is constrained all the time by its Treaty-base.

Subsidiarity means that certain powers may be repatriated where they have not been used by the Community or where it is no longer evident that they can be better exercised by the Community. The British government, which came late to the notion of subsidiarity, has appeared to wish to deploy it not just to decentralise the Community but also to slow down and in some cases to reverse European integration. Subsidiarity is, however, a two-edged sword: although it weakens the argument for supranational action in some cases it strengthens it in others. One of the tasks of the IGC should be to consider where the balance of advantage lies in different fields; and this has to be done against the background of the existing institutional arrangements. What subsidiarity is emphatically not is a licence for governments to choose at random between the intergovernmental and the Community method.

Existing institutions: strengths and weaknesses

The European Community shares the sovereignty of its member states and peoples according to the rule of law.

Its supreme arbiter is the European Court of Justice; it has common political institutions in the European Parliament, Commission and Council; it has a European Monetary Institute which is the precursor of a European Central Bank. The Commission, which acts as guarantor of the Treaties, can and does sue the member states for alleged infringement of them.[23] Moreover, all the EC institutions may take action in the Court of Justice against each other for infringement or failure to act. EC law is directly applicable inside the member states. The Community has its own financial resources. In establishing a common trade policy, customs union and internal market, and in working towards a single currency and common defence policy, the EC's mission is to unite the member states. Moreover after Maastricht, the Union has formally established a common European citizenship, uniting the citizens not as a substitute for nationality but as a supplement to it.

Nevertheless, the dimension of EU government remains small. Its most likely destination is not a single state but a union of states and peoples. Analogy with the USA is misleading: the member states come to the Union immeasurably more individualistic and powerful (and old) than those that formed the American federation, and they will continue to deploy much greater executive and legislative powers. The European Union will neither act nor look like the United States of America.

This is mainly because the Council, although an EC institution itself, is such a powerful mechanism for the protection of states' rights. Member states' governments and parliaments retain many important powers such as control of the ceiling to the Community's own financial resources and revision of the Treaties. They have also formalised the summit meetings of their heads of state or government together with the President of the Commission in the European Council, a powerful if erratic body that exercises some general strategic oversight over the work programme of the Council of ministers and the Commission.

Furthermore, some of the more federal elements of the Community's institutions do not so far apply to the Union's internal or external security policy. Here, the member states have guarded jealously their historic prerogatives. Of the three 'pillars' in the Maastricht Treaty, only the first, the EC, gives real powers to the more federal of the institutions: the European Parliament, Commission and Court of Justice. The second deals by intergovernmental diplomacy with common foreign and security policy. The third deals by similar methods with justice and interior affairs.

Even the Community, however, and despite the success of the structural funds, is weak in fiscal terms: the development over forty years of the Community method has not led to the build up of very wide or significant budgetary powers. The EC budget is planned to grow from 1.20% of Community GDP in 1994 to 1.27% in 1999 — compared to the nearly 50% of GDP spent on average by governments in the member states. Of that budget, half is spent on only 5% of the working population (farmers and fishermen), and another third is spent on only that quarter of the Union's population that happens to live in the depressed or peripheral regions and is eligible for structural funds.

Undemocratic

The European Community is not yet very democratic. First, the Commission does not have the strength to act like a fully-fledged parliamentary government; moreover, it is neither obviously elected nor clearly accountable. Second, the dominant Council of ministers passes EC law behind closed doors and without a proper published record; and in some important areas the Council legislates by itself, without the participation of the European Parliament. The exact position is over-complicated: in some fields the Council ignores the Parliament, in others consults it, or cooperates with it, or has to seek its assent, or, finally, and after conciliation, shares with it the power of co-decision. The Council, moreover, still works too much by unanimity, a method which makes decision-taking slow and often means that a democratic majority cannot progress the business of the Community, but is compelled to accept a minimal consensus. There is still a tendency in the Council to fail to discriminate between its executive and legislative roles, and for the ministers to treat matters as if they were foreign policy, with the result that everything is reduced to the politics of the lowest common denominator. In these circumstances the European Parliament feels itself to be, and is, the inferior partner. The result is a continuing constitutional struggle between the Parliament, which claims to represent the shared sovereignty of the peoples of Europe, and the Council, wherein rests the sovereignty of the states.

Nowhere is the struggle more crucially engaged than in the constituent process itself. The drafting of Treaty revisions leaves much to be desired. Previous IGCs have been conducted entirely in conclave by member state functionaries attended by the Commission, punctuated by some inter-institutional consultations (including one controversial *assises* in November 1990 made up of MPs and MEPs), and spiced by off-the-record briefings of the Brussels press corps. After their work is done, it falls to the member states' governments and parliaments alone, sometimes sanctioned by national referenda, to bring the changes into effect: the European Parliament is entirely excluded from the ratification process. It is certain that greater democracy will be achieved by greater transparency and a broader dialogue. The public reaction to Maastricht shows that this applies not least to the IGC process itself.

Here, then, is the central battleground of the forthcoming IGC, and it is a battle that has been enlivened by the recent and, in many places, continuing assertion of European popular sovereignty against the state in those false People's Republics of Communist Europe. Since 1989 the European Community can be complacent no longer about the state of its own parliamentary democracy.

There are currently twelve different ways in which the Community may take a decision. It is hardly surprising that it is not working very well. The European Commission is forced to share some of its executive power with the Council through a complex and controversial system of regulatory, management and advisory committees ('comitology').[24] The Commission lacks the powers and resources to ensure the full and effective implementation of EC policy; fraud, smuggling and bureaucratic bungling are not uncommon; and decisions on EC spending, faced with powerful national and sectional interests, are not always economically efficient. A comprehensive system of justice in the Union is still evolving, and 'fair play' is not always assured. Parliamentary scrutiny of executive decisions is inadequate and, as we have seen, legislative power is shared in a confused manner between Council and Parliament. In budgetary matters, Parliament has powers only over payments and not receipts. Who speaks for the Union in external relations is muddled between Commission and Council presidency.

All these problems of democracy and efficiency within the Community are accentuated by the existence of the two other pillars of the European Union. The common foreign and security policy of Maastricht is being tested and found wanting: it is badly aligned with the external economic policies of the EC and singularly ill-equipped to build an incisive strategy to deal with instability in Eastern Europe. The mismatch between the Union's aspirations in foreign and security policy and its foreign policy machinery has been exposed tragically in Bosnia-Herzegovina. But it is not only foreigners who suffer the consequences of the Union's weakness. Under the third pillar, police and security service cooperation is being developed beyond the reach of parliamentary control and, in most instances, of effective judicial remedies. The roles of the Commission and of the Parliament in both internal and external security matters are very restricted and the Court of Justice has virtually no role at all.

Above all, however, the profile of the governance of the Union is blurred and indistinct — the opposite, in fact, of what is required by the public interest. Distances from Brussels, geographical and psychological, can be very great, and, while EU government need not be of large dimensions, its outline must be sharp and clearly visible. Unfortunately, however, the history of post-war European integration has caused one treaty to be piled on top of another in an increasingly obscurantist way. There is an obvious danger that the IGC of 1996 may exacerbate the problem. It is essential, therefore, that citizens of the European Union soon begin to learn how they are governed, by whom and from where. The Union now requires a real and well-written constitution. Such a constitution should simplify and clarify the politics of executive power and the legislative and judicial processes for the sake of democracy, efficiency and respect for the rule of law.

European democracy requires such clarity of structure, served by a first-class public administration, nurtured by civic education with a strong European dimension and supported by a political class that will speak the truth about the scope and depth of the European Union. It requires the empowerment of the European citizen.

Strategic imperatives

What circumstances will prevail in 1996?[25] In retrospect, the timing of the European Council at Maastricht, in December 1991, looks most fortuitous: such a treaty agreement could have been achieved neither beforehand nor afterwards. A year earlier, having learned her lesson over the Single Act, Margaret Thatcher would not have signed the Maastricht Treaty. In her view, Maastricht develops Europe in a federal direction and such a Europe will be dominated by Germany. With partial justification, she wrote: 'Far too much of the Community's history had consisted of including nebulous phrases in treaties and communiqués, then later clothing them with federal meaning which we had been assured they never possessed'.[26] And a year after Maastricht, Western Europe was in deep economic recession. In September 1992 and August 1993 the Exchange Rate Mechanism (ERM) suffered speculative attacks that blew away any complacency about the eventual achievement of the central prize of Maastricht, Economic and Monetary Union. Meanwhile, in Central and Eastern Europe the brutish character of the communist legacy was completely exposed; the Soviet Union disintegrated and, in the Balkans, Croatia and Serbia began to dismantle Bosnia-Herzegovina. Pessimism had firmly set in. No wonder the ratification of the

Maastricht Treaty was so problematic, and that its coming into force was delayed for ten months in 1993. Constitution-mongering went quickly out of fashion.

A notable contemporary achievement, of course, is to have completed, more or less, the enlargement of the Union within Western Europe. This has been done without radical institutional reform of the EC itself, although the new Commission (at twenty members) is too big. The assimilation of the five East German Länder after October 1990 and the accession of Austria, Finland and Sweden in January 1995 creates a Union of fifteen states and 370 million people. The latter enlargement has been relatively straightforward in technical and economic terms, and has commanded popular assent by referendum despite widespread public apprehension of the real political implications of integration. Even military cooperation, through WEU or Partnership for Peace, may now be acceptable to these formerly neutral states. Those countries that choose to remain outside the Union — Iceland, Norway and Switzerland — do so for their own idiosyncratic reasons and pose neither a strategic problem for the Union nor a serious impediment to deeper European integration. Should they change their minds in the future, doubtless they would be welcomed into the Union.

The Union's European policy

The recent enlargement of the Union was greatly facilitated by the transformation of the European security situation that followed the fall of the Berlin Wall on 9 November 1989. That dramatic event and its consequences shape Europe's destiny, and it is they which, above all other, drive the agenda of the IGC of 1996. In marked contrast to the agenda of Maastricht, therefore, where preoccupations were almost entirely internal to the affairs of the Community, what matters most now is the Union's European policy.

Central Europe

The 'Visegrad Four' of Poland, Hungary, the Czech Republic and Slovakia are apparently committed to full membership of the Union at the earliest possible opportunity, and will be impatient on-lookers at the IGC. Bulgaria, Romania and Slovenia may not be far behind.[27] For these countries the prospect of unification with the West seems

14

attractive in economic terms; but it is imperative in terms of security. For neither the Conference on Security and Cooperation in Europe (CSCE), the North Atlantic Cooperation Council (NACC) nor Nato's new Partnership for Peace scheme (comprising joint military exercises on a bilateral basis with former Warsaw Pact countries) are wholly adequate responses to Central and Eastern Europe's sense of instability. The prospect of full membership of Nato on its own would provoke Russia and weaken Nato itself. Having been conceived to guarantee the collective defence of Western Europe, there is a danger that the more stretched Nato becomes to the East the looser it will become to the West. While future US administrations may agree to maintain up to 100,000 troops in Western Europe, they are scarcely likely to risk American soldiers in combat on Eastern Europe's frayed edges. On the assumption that Western Europe is to maintain a strong defence capability, if it is not possible to build up the European pillar of Nato, Nato itself will soon cease to be functional and some other trans-Atlantic organisation specifically including the EU will need to be created. That is why President Clinton has reinforced US support for continued European integration.

The alternative is to expand Nato but only in line with an enlarging EU that has incorporated WEU. That option is less likely to antagonise Russia and more likely to evoke a positive response from the USA. For the United States of America the obvious choice of partner is a united Europe. That American message has a particular resonance in Germany which has been the first member state to welcome enlargement of the Union towards Central Europe. The British government expresses its commitment to the same goal. The French seem to have accepted the further enlargement as inevitable. Therefore, even if the Germans and the British continue to have diametrically opposed views about the kind of Union they want to see (with the French somewhere in the middle), but all three governments are agreed on its size, it is reasonable to assume that, in less than a decade from now, the European Union will have grown to include at least Poland, Hungary and the Czech Republic, with perhaps Slovakia, Slovenia, Bulgaria, Romania and the three Baltic states not far behind.

As we have already suggested, such a large Union will not work if it continues to be run on intergovernmental lines: current inefficiencies would be magnified and common policy would be reduced to the lowest possible consensus. Moreover, Germany's size, strength and strategic position would cause it to dominate an intergovernmental Europe. Contrary to the Thatcher thesis, it is only a European Union that is itself based on the principles of liberal democracy, including the rule of law and representative government, that can subsume the power politics of the old nation states.

Security

If the IGC is to plan sensibly for future enlargement, it must make the necessary preparations to strengthen the institutions of the Union and to enhance its democratic credentials. But it will also have to provide the ways and means to implement an effective European security policy. The options are numerous for the EU and WEU, and a priority for 1996 is to settle their relationship. On the assumption that the IGC will not agree that the European Community is capable of running its own foreign and defence policy along supranational lines, should WEU be wound up inside the EU's second, intergovernmental pillar? [28] If WEU successfully develops the use of Combined Joint Task Forces inside Nato (but excluding US and Canadian forces), should these find their way directly into the revised EU Treaty? Despite the initially contemptuous reaction of the UK, has the Eurocorps, with potentially 40,000 heavy-armoured troops, a useful military function, and, if so, how should it be constituted? [29] And, as we speculate above, to what extent should there be a firm twinning between extending Nato guarantees and enlarging EU/WEU membership?

For those East European countries for whom full EU accession is inappropriate, it should be possible to work out a cogent and multi-faceted partnership arrangement which both respects Russia's sphere of influence and builds up economic and political relations with the Union. As far as Russia is concerned, the CSCE is a useful — and, by the West, undervalued — tool. The isolation of Russia by the West would be imprudent, and its ostracism disastrous. A refurbished CSCE acting as the regional arm of the United Nations would allow Russia and the European Union to develop a useful diplomatic partnership by working together over a whole range of practical political and security issues. Moreover, the USA's active participation in CSCE would to some extent reassure Turkey and those in the CIS who oppose Russian hegemony.

16

Since 1989 the Western allies have shown considerable ingenuity in the way they have tackled the unexpected liberalisation of communist Europe. In both economics (the 'Europe Agreements') and security matters (NACC, Partnership for Peace) new arrangements have been created wherever old ones have proved inadequate and inflexible. Habits are changing swiftly, not only perforce in the ex-Soviet bloc, but also in the West: France is abandoning its poised semi-detachment from Nato in the military field; Britain is warming to the idea of a European pillar in Nato; Germany is preparing to send troops abroad; of the neutral countries, Finland and Sweden are moving on-side; Austria and Ireland are considering their position. The IGC should catch this spirit of innovation and look beyond the rhetoric of national politicians to what is already happening in Europe—and to what will be really needed to ensure its security and that of its neighbours in the future.

Mediterranean

Already in the pipeline are the outstanding membership applications from Cyprus and Malta, whose accession would have significant consequences for both the Union's institutional procedures and its Mediterranean policy. The prospect of such mini-states assuming the presidency of the Council, for example, is to say the least intriguing; and the extension of the Union's orbit to the shores of the Middle East and the Maghreb would imply a willingness on behalf of the Union to shoulder new strategic responsibilities. Cyprus, moreover, carries with it the intractable problem of Turkey.

Europe should no longer neglect the strategic predicament of Turkey, a highly unstable country with a troubled democracy, which is a Nato partner and about to enter a customs union with the EU. The size of the country commands respect: Istanbul is already Europe's largest city. Moreover, Turkey's vital strategic interests in the Middle East, in the CIS and, potentially, in the Balkans affect Europe directly.

Nevertheless, despite its long-standing application, Turkish accession to the Union is nowadays an unrealistic proposition, although a continued policy of sustained inactivity in the relations between the two would be unhelpful. Germany, especially, which is host to 1.8 million Turkish migrant workers, cannot let EU relations with

17

Turkey stagnate. Neither Greek irredentism nor Turkey's volatile economy should be erected as barriers to closer cooperation between Brussels and Ankara.[30] While negotiations for Turkish accession cannot at present be countenanced, the Union should make every effort to ensure that a suitable partnership is achieved.

The establishment on a sound footing of the Union's Mediterranean policy also requires giving urgent attention to the Maghreb, which is turbulent and poor. France, Spain and Italy have strong ties with and large immigrant populations from those countries. What happens in Morocco or Algeria has consequences throughout the Moslem world and will affect the whole raft of European relations with the Middle East. So Europe has a problem: the question is, will the European Union treat instability in the Mediterranean area as a common problem, or will member states, acting alone, attempt to shuffle off responsibilities? The IGC has a chance to facilitate a common approach to the Mediterranean.

Civilian Europe

The assumption of powers in the military field might jeopardise the EU's status and reputation as a civilian power. The implications for the Union's internal development are serious. Clearly, no credible system of political command and control of integrated armed forces could be established in a European Union that lacked a discernible central government made wholly accountable to representative institutions enjoying democratic legitimacy. A fully-fledged European federal democracy is a prerequisite to a full integration of armed forces. Indeed, it would be difficult to accept further European integration in the area of external security unless it is subject to stronger and more democratic institutions.

Likewise with internal security. At present the third pillar of Maastricht establishes a framework inside which ad hoc, intergovernmental conventions (some of them secret) affecting police, customs and judicial affairs can be cobbled up between member states and beyond the reach of both national and the European parliaments. The issues are far from marginal, involving as they do immigration, asylum, extradition, deportation, the fight against the Mafia and political terrorism, drug trafficking, financial and computer fraud, and smuggling. Within the Union, moreover, a core of member

18

states (excluding the UK, Ireland and Denmark) have signed the Schengen Agreement which seeks to make the freedom of movement of peoples a reality while erecting effective common police and customs controls. Concern about the erosion of civil liberties coupled with problems of computer software delayed the coming into force of Schengen until Spring 1995.[31] But it is hard to escape the conclusion that progress will soon have to be made within the EU Treaty in harmonising the interior affairs of the member states in an open and democratic manner, fully respecting subsidiarity. [SEE TABLE TWO]

TABLE TWO

INTERNAL SECURITY COOPERATION AND INTEGRATION

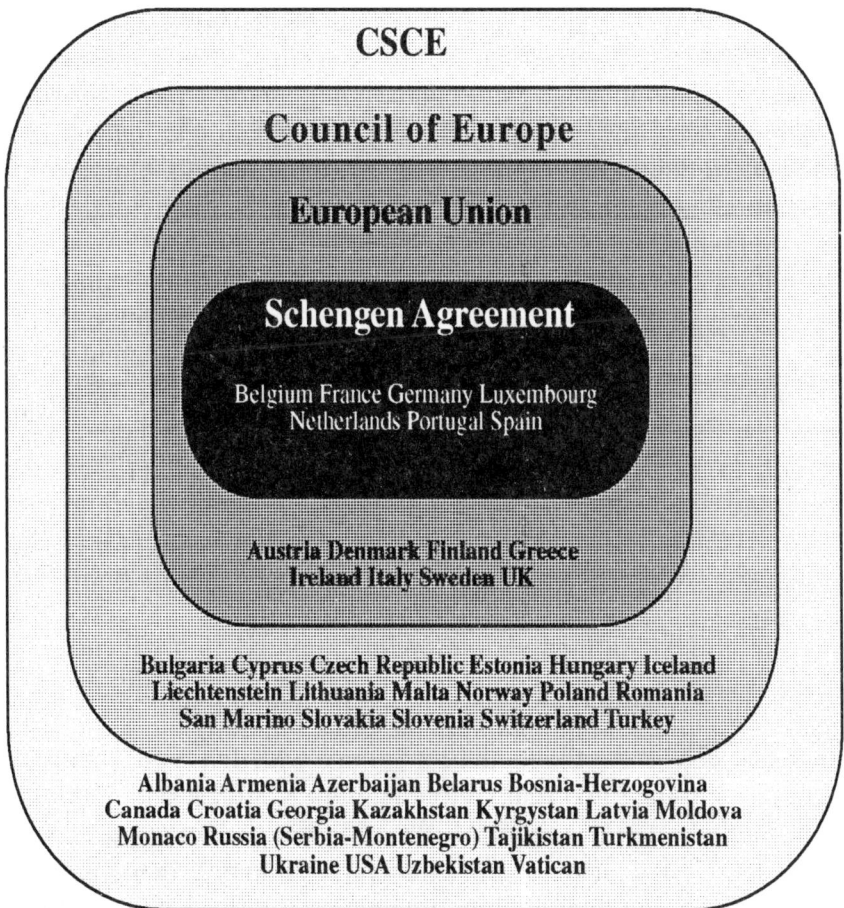

CSCE

Council of Europe

European Union

Schengen Agreement

Belgium France Germany Luxembourg
Netherlands Portugal Spain

Austria Denmark Finland Greece
Ireland Italy Sweden UK

Bulgaria Cyprus Czech Republic Estonia Hungary Iceland
Liechtenstein Lithuania Malta Norway Poland Romania
San Marino Slovakia Slovenia Switzerland Turkey

Albania Armenia Azerbaijan Belarus Bosnia-Herzogovina
Canada Croatia Georgia Kazakhstan Kyrgystan Latvia Moldova
Monaco Russia (Serbia-Montenegro) Tajikistan Turkmenistan
Ukraine USA Uzbekistan Vatican

Macedonia

Greece and Italy have signed the Schengen Agreement but have not implemented it.

19

These issues raise an interesting dilemma for the United Kingdom. It is in the national interest, defined on a bi-partisan basis, that the UK plays a prominent part in any European security arrangement. By the standards of contemporary Europe, Britain is both well-ordered in civilian terms and a strong military power. It maintains a large professional army, navy and air force and is prepared to deploy them, and it is still a significant player in the armaments and aerospace industries. The UK has no inhibitions about the dispatch of its troops around the globe: indeed, following withdrawal from Hong Kong in 1997 and troop reductions on the Rhine and in Northern Ireland, there may be a shortage of possible places to station UK armed forces. It would be wholly credible, therefore, for Britain to look to play a high-profile military role within the new Europe and on behalf of Europe elsewhere in the world. The questions, however, of who is to afford to subsidise the cost of a future British military contribution on the European mainland and overseas, and under what terms and conditions British armed forces are to be sent to war, cannot be resolved satisfactorily within any of the existing concentric international organisations. [SEE TABLE THREE]

The IGC of 1996 is obliged by the Treaty of Maastricht to reconsider the security and defence dimension of the European Union. It is likely that the Union itself will emerge from this reassessment with reinforced competences in this field. As they contemplate the IGC, therefore, British ministers must be asking themselves whether it is possible to opt into the 'hard core' of a defence Union but to opt out of a monetary Union — or for that matter of a future police and passport Union. They will be all too well aware that some of the UK's partners are reluctant to accept such an arrangement of 'variable geometry'.

Multi-speed Europe

There is much loose talk about how to cope with divergence within the context of the European Union. Helmut Kohl has said that it is not possible for the EU convoy to travel at the speed of the slowest. But that, of course, is precisely what convoys do: it is in the nature of convoys that the slowest ships are not allowed to fall behind. The Chancellor might have said that those who are willing to travel but weak need help and protection, whereas those who are unwilling to continue had better leave the convoy altogether.

20

TABLE THREE

EXTERNAL SECURITY AND DEFENCE
COOPERATION AND INTEGRATION

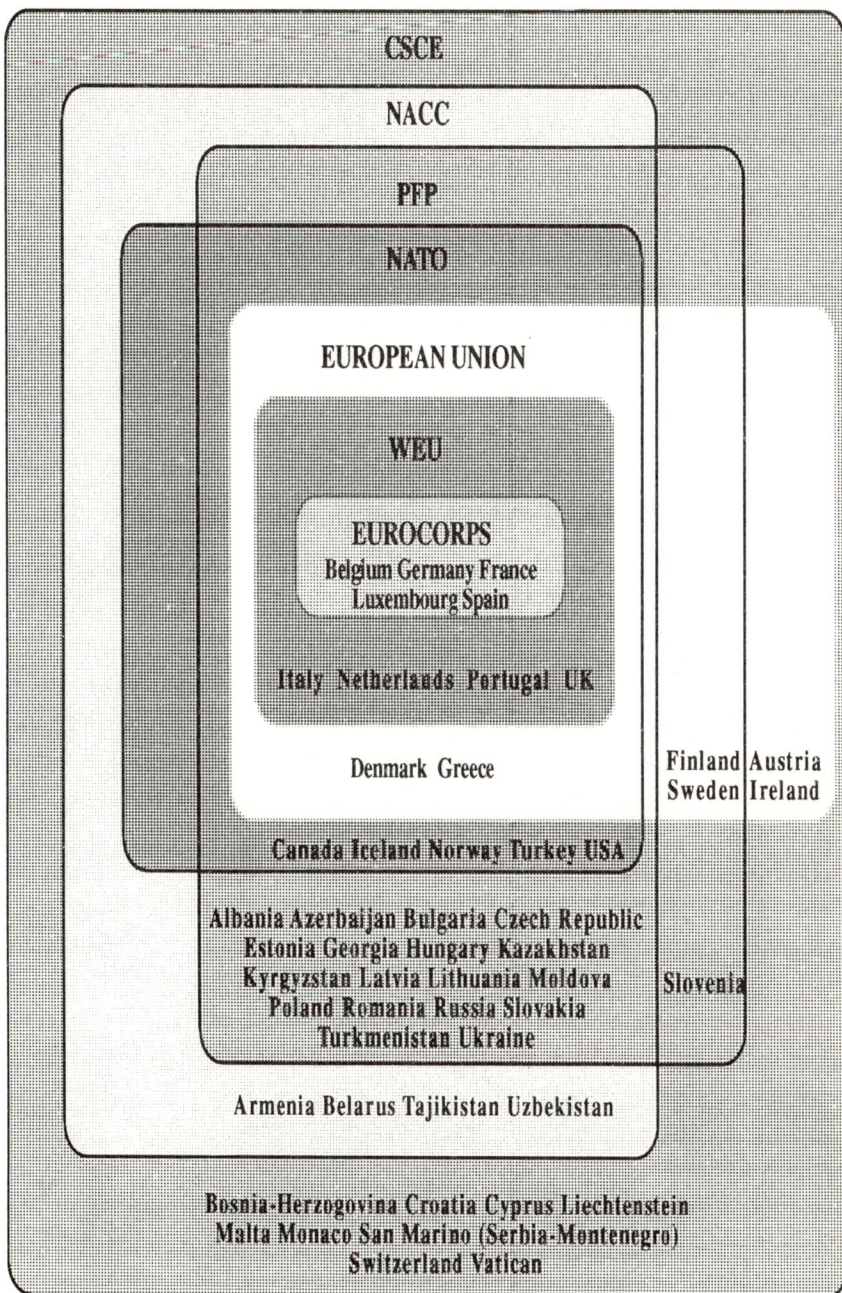

CSCE

NACC

PFP

NATO

EUROPEAN UNION

WEU

EUROCORPS
Belgium Germany France
Luxembourg Spain

Italy Netherlands Portugal UK

Denmark Greece   Finland Austria
                                  Sweden Ireland

Canada Iceland Norway Turkey USA

Albania Azerbaijan Bulgaria Czech Republic
Estonia Georgia Hungary Kazakhstan
Kyrgyzstan Latvia Lithuania Moldova   Slovenia
Poland Romania Russia Slovakia
Turkmenistan Ukraine

Armenia Belarus Tajikistan Uzbekistan

Bosnia-Herzogovina Croatia Cyprus Liechtenstein
Malta Monaco San Marino (Serbia-Montenegro)
Switzerland Vatican

Macedonia

21

John Major has talked equally confusingly of the notion of a 'multi-speed, multi-tier, multi-layer' Europe. There is a distinction between a 'multi-speed' Europe and a 'multi-tier' or 'multi-layer' Europe. 'Multi-speed' implies that member states are pursuing common objectives but for reasons of economic circumstance — or, exceptionally, of political disposition — are achieving different rates of progress. This is a fairly common feature of the European Community. Every previous enlargement of the EC, for example, has witnessed quite long transition periods after accession before the full force of the acquis communautaire applied to the new member states. In some cases, albeit lamentable, such as with Italian milk quotas, special dispensation is granted by the Council to a member state when the full and proper implementation of EC law proves to be beyond its capability. In other cases, the effect of common policy is deliberately postponed. That the UK will not have to apply the full force of the EC Directive on working hours for several years after its partners have done so is such an example of a concession wrung from the Council by the stubbornness of one government.

More respectably, the Treaty of Maastricht introduces one very important element of 'multi-speed' into the development of Economic and Monetary Union. While the principle of EMU was agreed at Maastricht, there remain many important practical decisions to be taken in 1996 and beyond, especially concerning the working of the European System of Central Banks and the arrangements for replacing national currencies with the Ecu. Under the terms of the Treaty, in December 1996 the European Council is obliged to decide whether a majority of member states have fulfilled the convergence criteria and are ready to go forward to Stage Three of EMU and to adopt the single currency.[32] If within one year the heads of government cannot agree on fixing a date for the transition to Stage Three, it will begin anyway in 1999 with as many member states as are willing and able participating (but not necessarily a majority). Once other member states are deemed to have achieved convergence, they will join up to the single currency. Similarly, when newly acceding member states achieve the threshold, they too will be deemed to have subscribed to the club rules for senior membership. In short, we have the prospect of a relatively orderly progression to full EMU, state by state, as and when the stipulated convergence of inflation, interest rates, public deficits and exchange rates is attained. [SEE TABLE FOUR]

ECONOMIC COOPERATION AND INTEGRATION

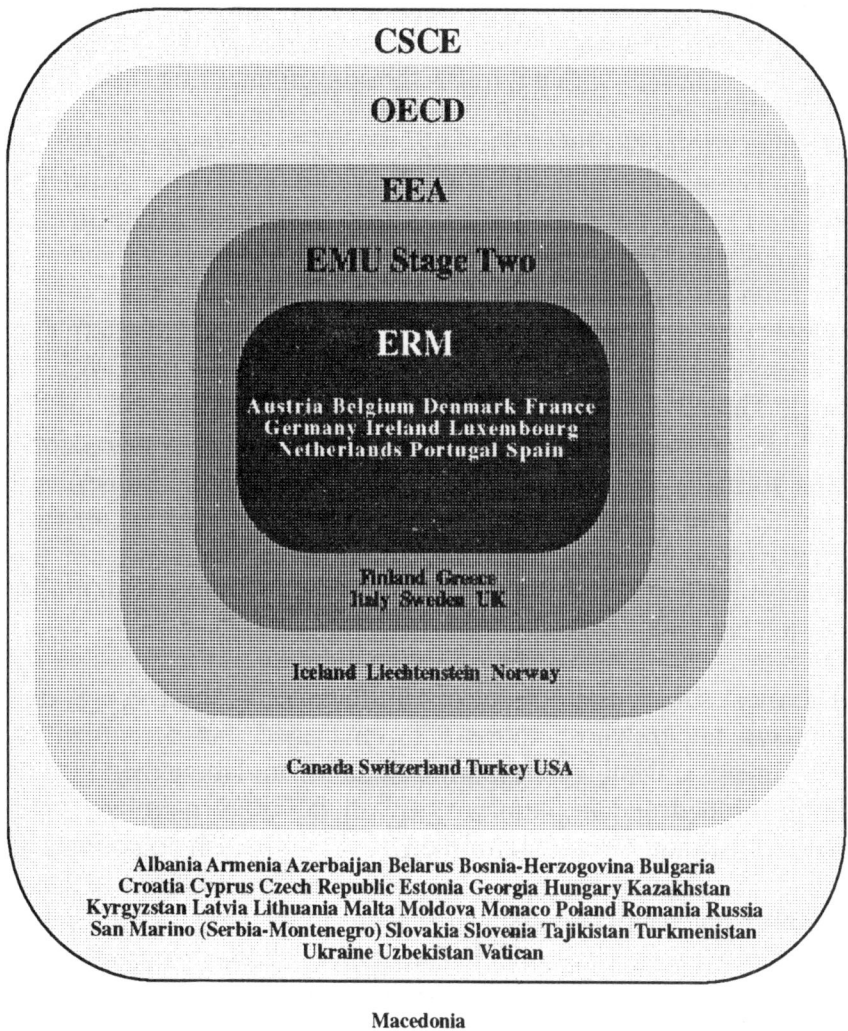

CSCE

OECD

EEA

EMU Stage Two

ERM

Austria Belgium Denmark France
Germany Ireland Luxembourg
Netherlands Portugal Spain

Finland Greece
Italy Sweden UK

Iceland Liechtenstein Norway

Canada Switzerland Turkey USA

Albania Armenia Azerbaijan Belarus Bosnia-Herzogovina Bulgaria
Croatia Cyprus Czech Republic Estonia Georgia Hungary Kazakhstan
Kyrgyzstan Latvia Lithuania Malta Moldova Monaco Poland Romania Russia
San Marino (Serbia-Montenegro) Slovakia Slovenia Tajikistan Turkmenistan
Ukraine Uzbekistan Vatican

Macedonia

For the sake of consistency, only Canada, the USA and the European members of OECD are shown.

Multi-tier Europe

The Schengen Agreement is one clear example of a multi-tier Europe. More controversial, however, is the fact that first the UK and then Denmark wrung concessions from their partners in the matter of Economic and Monetary Union which were not of the nature of temporary derogation but of a permanent right to opt out. In so doing they were further accentuating the variable geometry of the Union and reinforcing 'multi-tier' Europe. In a Protocol attached to the Treaty, the UK is allowed to take a unilateral decision in its own time about whether it shall take part in the move to Stage Three of EMU (on the presumption that it fulfils the convergence criteria).

Another Protocol gives Denmark the right to exempt itself from Stage Three, a derogation that was later reinforced at the insistence of the Danish political parties as they concocted a package to persuade the Danish people to change their negative referendum decision on the Maastricht Treaty. That 'national compromise', which was accepted by the European Council at Edinburgh in December 1992, declared that Denmark would not participate in Stage Three.[33] Another derogation was then added by the Danes to include common defence policy, and the whole 'set of arrangements' was formally adopted by the Council. During the subsequent (positive) referendum campaign, the package was incorrectly portrayed as being of indefinite duration: in fact, however, the European Council had insisted that it be put up for renegotiation in the IGC of 1996.

The most substantial opt-out of all, however, is the UK's Social Protocol under whose terms it is envisaged that a number of measures establishing minimum standards in the labour market may be developed and implemented by all the other member states without Britain.[34] The risk for the UK is that British companies to whom the stipulations apply because of their operations in other member states will choose in any case to adopt them for the sake of uniformity of corporate policy. The risk for the other member states is that the UK derogation will disrupt the supposedly 'level playing field' of the single market and corrupt the integrity of EC law. Certainly the Social Protocol has encumbered the Community with yet more procedural and institutional problems, and the view is strongly held in many quarters that it and similar derogations should only be temporary.[35] Moreover, it is a paradox that the more derogations there are from the common rules, the tighter the supervision of the market by government has to become in order to preserve the integrity of the regime. As mutual trust loosens in a union, central regulation must tighten if the project is not to fall apart.

It is important to draw the right lessons from the precedent set by the Social Protocol. On the one hand, Europe *à la carte*, a feast where members are completely free to pick and choose what appears to suit them at the time, is not a sound basis for continued European integration. On the other hand, a sophisticated network of variable arrangements where member states negotiate derogations from non-essential aspects of EU policy may be unavoidable.

The problem, of course, is to identify an agreed definition of core competences from which no opt-out is admissible and where implementation of policy is strictly enforced by the Commission and the Court inside all member states. Many of the core areas are self-evident, such as customs union, common commercial policy, competition policy, budget and single market. Some traditional areas of EC common policy, such as agricultural price support, may not now be essential as long as the single agricultural market is assured and workers have sufficient common rights to guarantee the 'level playing field'. Other areas, notably some aspects of tax harmonisation, monetary, foreign and security policies, will be more contentious, while yet others, such as environment policy, may be left to the strict application of subsidiarity.

At the heart of the problem of definition is the political culture of the Council of ministers which spawns spurious definitions of national interest. Even in well-established fields of common policy, like agriculture, the importance of sectional interests far outweighs that of national interests. The aspirations and anxieties of Welsh hill farmers, for example, have more in common with those of their counterparts in the Pyrenees than with their compatriot arable farmers from East Anglia. This disjunction between 'national' and group interest is even more far-reaching in new sectors of common policy, for example in the social or environmental fields. These areas are still treated by the Council as if they were foreign policy despite the self-evident fact that within the domestic context of British politics there is no agreement on what constitutes good social policy: indeed, there is marked disagreement both between the political parties and the social partners, and between regions. Once in Brussels, however, in the equally legitimate debate on social policy within the European dimension, the UK government (which, incidentally, is always elected on a minority vote) is regarded as speaking unequivocally for Britain. This contrivance means that EC public policy may often be driven by short-term, domestic electoral considerations. It is not difficult to see that, when followed to a logical conclusion, this approach might end with an explosion of national opt-outs and cop-outs that would serve only to weaken the Union.

German leadership

Not before time, the Germans have begun to instil a more disciplined approach to the debate about variable geometry within the Union. In a paper published in September 1994, the CDU/CSU parliamentary party set out a deliberately provocative proposal for a 'hard core' of states to exercise a centripetal or magnetic effect on the whole Union.[36] The paper's authors, Wolfgang Schäuble and Karl Lamers, advance five mutually dependent proposals:

- developing European federal democracy;
- strengthening the hard core;
- deepening Franco-German integration;
- improving the Union's capacity for action in foreign and security policy;
- expanding the Union towards the East.

Naturally, the second point has received the most publicity. But the priority for the Germans is the federal project and the application of the principle of subsidiarity. This applies not only to the division of powers between the government of the EU and the member states, but also to the question of 'whether public authorities, including those of the Union, should perform certain functions or leave them to groups in society'. With regard to the institutions of the Union, Schäuble and Lamers follow the classical prescriptions of the European federalist movement, notably as set out in Altiero Spinelli's Draft Treaty of European Union that had been adopted by the European Parliament in 1984.[37] In other words, in a final constitutional settlement, the Commission is elevated to the status of parliamentary government, and the Council and Parliament become co-equal partners of a bicameral legislature.

A stronger and more democratic Union is required to cope with EMU as well as with the strains of enlargement to the East. For

Germany, as a close neighbour of Central and East European countries, this is a particular interest. But it is an interest shared by other member states, and Schäuble and Lamers would prefer that all of them should accept the necessary reforms at the 1996 IGC. It is pessimism about the prospects for this that drives them to propose a multi-tier approach to the development of the Union. Article N of the Treaty of Maastricht that concerns its revision requires unanimity. The net result of seeking and achieving a consensus among the current member states is all too likely to be minimal progress towards these German objectives. Replacement of the unanimity rule, therefore, by some form of qualified majority voting seems to the CDU/CSU to be an inevitable consequence.

The message is clear: neither the British nor anyone else can be allowed to block the federal process; partnership between Germany, France and Benelux must continue to deepen, particularly in some policy areas where the EC won new competences at Maastricht — that is, those pertaining to the creation of an ultra-modern and competitive information society; Stage Three of EMU must be reached as quickly as possible: here the hard core of five member states could be joined by Denmark, Ireland, Finland, Austria and Sweden.

Schäuble and Lamers went on to insist that the Franco-German relationship remains at the crux of the Union. The traditional Gaullist (and now Thatcherite) vision of a loose association of European states extending far to the East gives rise, not least in Germany, to widespread fears of German hegemony. France should therefore 'rectify the impression that, although it allows no doubt as to its basic will to pursue European integration, it often hesitates in taking concrete steps towards this objective'. In defence as in economic matters, the 'frequent divergence of views' between the two countries must be overcome. The failure of the Common Foreign and Security Policy arrangements of Maastricht in the Balkans has led to a dangerous level of public disillusion with the Union itself. 'The creation of a common European defence is a matter of much greater urgency than envisaged in the Maastricht Treaty. It should be done now, rather than "in time" as stated in the Treaty.'[38] Similarly, the staged enlargement of the EU to include Central Europe must be hastened.

The significance of the German initiative is undoubted, not least in that it makes analysis and prescription that were once the preserve of academic debate the common currency of EU politics. Its importance was enhanced by the re-election in October 1994 of Chancellor Kohl, who is undoubtedly sympathetic to the general drift of his colleagues' paper, even if he would not support it in every respect. It also has an unmistakable message for British European policy: the UK is not a priority for Germany. In a speech at Leiden in September, however, the British Prime Minister reacted against the German proposals for a federal core, missing the point about essential German interests, and casting doubt on the legitimacy of the European Parliament and the validity of the Community method:

'The determination of the Founding Fathers has succeeded far beyond the estimations of most people of their time. Their vision was proved right for its age. But it is outdated, it will not do now. We must all adjust our vision to meet the challenges of today and tomorrow'.[39]

But understandably, the vision of Jean Monnet and the other Founding Fathers still seems good to very many people, particularly in the founding member states. The problem is, therefore, that although the UK would no doubt be welcomed 'at the heart of Europe', to get there British politicians have to drop the semi-detached and rather arrogant attitude that many of them still adopt, and instead engage fully in the mainstream, mainland political debate. As Lamers retorted, 'Those who, like John Major, in principle accept the method of variable geometry can neither object to nor prevent the formation of a hard core'.[40]

The German government has drawn its political conclusions from the October 1993 judgement of the German Constitutional Court at Karlsruhe on the Treaty of Maastricht. In its otherwise favourable (although complicated and controversial) opinion, the Court was critical of the democratic legitimacy of the EU. Further European integration, it said, should not proceed in the absence of further democratisation and the reinforcement of European citizenship which established a 'legal connection' between the nationals of member states and articulated a commonality of democratic interest. The European Parliament was gaining in democratic authority, and would continue to do so especially if the Treaty were to be fully implemented in respect of electoral reform, but national parliaments would not fade away and must not be by-passed.[41] In fact, the Court recommended an increased role for the Bundestag in monitoring EC affairs, especially the progress of EMU.

How federal is the European Union?

In considering the German view of EU reform, the word federal can hardly be avoided, and indeed should not be, if the German position and that of many of the political forces in the Union are to be properly understood. But since the word has generated so much heat in British political debate, it seems necessary to state what we understand it to mean.

Federalism is the dispersal of power between separate authorities according to the rule of law. It is a constitutional method of enabling different states or communities, each one dealing with its own affairs according to the principles of liberal democracy, to live peaceably together and manage their common affairs with a federal government based on similar principles. In respect of powers held concurrently, these different levels of government must be coordinated with each other but no one level is subordinate to any other. In respect of powers fully transferred under the constitution, federal law has supremacy.

Seen in this light, the European Union has many of the characteristics of a federal system of government, although it is not yet fully democratic and not working very well — particularly in the pillars relating to internal and external security, which are considerably more intergovernmental than the Community itself. Discussion about the Union with our partners, and indeed within Britain, would be more constructive if federalism was understood in this way, rather than being obfuscated by slogans such as 'centralised superstate'.

Whereas traditional international relations, governed by consensus, tend to be based on the presumption that states mistrust each other, the development of a system governed by majoritarian decision-making has to be based on mutual trust. In the EU's Council of ministers there has always been a tussle between those who insist on unanimity wherever possible — thereby retaining a national veto —

and those of a more federalist persuasion who prefer the qualified majority vote. In March 1994, at Ioannina in Greece, the UK government demonstrated its distrust of its partners and the Community system by demanding that the relative size of the blocking minority in the Council should be lowered. At Ioannina a temporary compromise was reached, but it was also formally agreed that the issue of the weighting of votes in the Council and the threshold of the qualified majority should be added to the agenda of the 1996 IGC.[42] This question of balance in a federation between large and small states is an important matter, and was dodged at Maastricht. It becomes more important for the EU as the differential widens with enlargement and as variable types of integration require a variety of voting procedures.

Another indispensable quality of federal systems is solidarity between the different regions of the territory, or in usual EC parlance 'cohesion'. This has implied a redistribution of resources between member states and their regions through the medium of the 'structural funds' — now amounting to about a third of the total EC budget, or 0.4% of the Union's GNP. Such direct expenditure by the EC level of government has obvious, and mostly beneficial political consequences, not least on the effectiveness of eligible regional and local authorities who compete for EC funding. Clearly, for a decentralised system of government to work well, each level has to be as fit and as cooperative as the next.

Diverse reactions in France and Britain

The German initiative poses acute problems for France, whose government does not share the same federalist perspective but has, ever since the 1950s, been much more willing than that of the UK to go the extra kilometre to reach agreement with Germany. French priorities still seem to be threefold: to strengthen the ties that bind Germany into the Union, to protect the CAP and to enhance the power of the European Council. The first and by far the most fundamental can only be achieved by satisfying Germany over enlargement and by reducing the force of habitual French reservations about extending qualified majority voting in the Council and about strengthening the powers of the European Parliament. It is increasingly obvious, however, that enlargement to Central Europe, which is necessary to address the German question, will put paid to the CAP as we know it. With an unreformed CAP the budgetary consequences of the next enlargement are likely to be too heavy — perhaps a doubling of the total size of EC expenditure, with the ceiling on agricultural spending already raised to over 1.5% of EU GNP by the year 2000. Both France and the UK would be major donors. But despite such potential sources of strain, the Paris-Bonn relationship remains central to French policy. France and Germany are likely to reach an accommodation including the completion of EMU, the development of European defence capacity, stronger powers for the European Parliament and enlargement to Central Europe. Certainly there is no significant support in France for a minimalist IGC. Edouard Balladur has moreover given support to the idea of a European inner core by speaking of two tiers of full member states, as well as a third tier of 'partner states', including Russia and Turkey.[43] [SEE TABLE FIVE]

In the UK, by contrast, the debate about 1996 has scarcely begun. The popular press is nationalist and xenophobic; the Liberal Democrats lack weight; 'new Labour' is cautious on the old matter of Europe and rather quiet about the IGC; and the Conservatives are deeply split. If any British government succeeds in minimising the scope of the IGC, it will frustrate Germany: the IGC will then fail and Germany will seek to proceed with its friends, leaving Britain aside. If, as seems likely, such a core group is then established, Britain will once again face the invidious choice between isolation or the grudging acceptance of arrangements made by others. But if Germany's partners, and in particular France, fail to proceed with deeper integration, Germany will be driven to play an increasingly independent hand in Central and Eastern Europe as elsewhere, leading ineluctably to German hegemony and European instability. This runs so starkly counter to the interests of all Europe, including the British, that it is hard to credit that a UK government could risk provoking such an outcome by standing out against a reasonable minimum of reforms, for example greater legislative powers for the European Parliament.

It is, however, certainly possible for an IGC to fail. The European Defence Community was blocked in 1954 by a vote of the French parliament. The Treaty of Maastricht was saved in the end by a few thousand votes in national referenda and by three (Liberal Democrat) votes in the House of Commons.[44] All that is needed for a Treaty revision to fail is rejection by one of fifteen member states, some of whom are required to have a referendum and several of whom, including Britain, might choose to do so. The consequences would be grave. If the core group proceeds without it, Britain will be isolated. If the process of integration that has brought Europe to the greatest prosperity and stability that it has ever known is stopped and eventually reversed, the rest of Europe, as well as Britain, will suffer.

TABLE FIVE

EUROPE 2000

OSCE

EU Partner States

EU 2nd Tier

EU 1st Tier

Belgium France Germany
Luxembourg Netherlands

Austria Bulgaria Cyprus Czech Republic
Denmark Finland Greece Hungary
Iceland Ireland Italy Liechtenstein Malta
Norway Poland Portugal Romania
Slovakia Slovenia Spain Sweden UK

Albania Belarus Bosnia-Herzogovina Croatia
Estonia Georgia Latvia Lithuania Macedonia
Moldova Monaco Russia San Marino Switzerland
Turkey Ukraine Vatican

Armenia Azerbaijan Canada Kazakhstan Kyrgystan
Serbia-Montenegro Tajikstan Turkmenistan USA Uzbekistan

This table speculates about one possible configuration of Europe in five years time, on the conclusion of a federal constitutional settlement. The two-tiered EU has 27 members and a close economic and political partnership agreement with all the rest of Europe except Serbia. On the basis of their membership of the inner concentric circles in Tables Two, Three and Four, only 5 states really qualify for the inner tier here. The OSCE is the former CSCE.

Making a success of the IGC

We hope it will now be clear why we consider that the best result for the IGC will be achieved if all the member states agree on reforms that will substantially strengthen the Union and make it more democratic. We have to face the strong possibility, however, that a minority of member states, which might well include the UK, will want to resist such reforms and be tempted to block them.

A wise solution, therefore, is for all member states to accept proposals for the simultaneous deepening and widening of the Union even if they do not choose at this stage to participate in all aspects of the deeper integration. Such a strategy should accommodate both nationalists and federalists: nationalists can hardly object to the principle that other states do what they choose; federalists can expect the 'hard core' to grow in time and, meanwhile, to make progress towards the historic goals of the European Union. It is not beyond the bounds of the ingenuity of the IGC to devise mechanisms (EMU offers an example) so that the core group can remain within the Union and use the common institutions, and the member states in the outer ring have systematic opportunities to reconsider their position.

To achieve this delicate balancing act, however, the IGC in 1996 should concentrate on one or two constitutional reforms of fundamental importance. Indeed, the IGC will be sorely tempted to put off further some of the still unfinished business of Maastricht. As their provenance would indicate, some of these issues are very controversial, and not least those raised at Edinburgh in 1992 and at Ioannina in 1994.

In addition, and with the exception of further integration with respect to defence, it would be both unwise and unnecessary for the European Commission or the Parliament to push for the transfer of major new fields of competence to the Union. Maastricht gave the Union the powers it needs: the question for 1996 is how they should be exercised.[45]

The Constituent Process

Given the state of the Union today, it is highly unlikely that the forthcoming IGC will provide the new Europe with the federal constitution it needs. However, the 1996 IGC could prepare the way for the final constituent process and even programme its completion, perhaps to coincide with the future enlargement of the Union to Central Europe around the year 2000.

Unless all member states prove willing to accept reforms judged by a critical mass within the Union to be necessary, the priority for this IGC should be to forge agreement on changes to the way in which the Treaties are amended in order to allow for the formation of a more federal core in a way that does not disrupt excessively the acquis communautaire. In other words, 1996 should find methods of making variable geometry an acceptable condition of European integration. Some preliminary agreement must be reached on what comprises the essential core of rules and competences, the ties that bind all member states. And while those engaged in multi-speed aspects of integration should be encouraged to change gear and accelerate, those in outer tiers of integration would be enabled, sector by sector, to clamber towards the inner tier.

In our view, therefore, while we may continue to hope that all governments decide to move forward together, at the very least the 1996 IGC should try:

- to devise methods to enable core member states to proceed autonomously to deepen their own integration within the Union, as far as possible using the common institutions;

- to amend the Treaty on European Union to allow such a core to strengthen the institutional arrangements that apply among themselves without requiring the agreement of the other member states.

Ratification

Ratification of the results of the IGC will be much assisted by a drafting process that is both more public and more pluralistic than that leading up to Maastricht. The presence of two MEPs in the (possibly misnamed) Group of Reflection is a step in the right direction. But the IGC of 1996 should go further and seek to enlist the services of the European Parliament as a full member of any future IGC — to be renamed 'Constitutional Conference' — and to give to the Parliament as well as to national parliaments the power of ratification. The revised Article N would establish a new form of constituent assembly to revise the Treaty (along the lines of IGC + Parliament), and stipulate new procedures for ratifying the conclusions. The first step would be approval by a qualified majority vote of the Council of, say, two-thirds of member governments. The second step would be to acquire the assent of an absolute majority of the European Parliament. Ratification would then proceed, as now, in each member state according to domestic constitutional requirements. Lastly, it would be possible then to turn to the device of an EU-wide referendum.

Across Europe referenda spawn each other because there is great public disillusion with parties and parliaments. An element of direct democracy at the level of the European Union would compensate for the lowly status of the European Parliament and ensure the legitimation of the sovereign people as well as of the sovereign states to the new constituent process. An EU-wide referendum, with all the votes aggregated in one result, would seek to confirm the previous assent of the European Parliament by a simple majority. Any member state which, through its own domestic constitutional procedures, failed to achieve ratification for the proposed Treaty revisions, would then face the choice of having to leave the Union or to try again, as the Danes did in 1992-93, to get a positive national result.

In the end, therefore, it may be essential to consider supplementing these changes by the inclusion of a clause laying down the right of a member state to secede voluntarily from the Union (none exists at present) according to a new constitutional procedure.

In the same spirit, Article O of the Treaty might be amended to end the right of unilateral national veto to the enlargement of the Union.

Other measures

To prepare the Parliament for these significantly increased constituent responsibilities, and to improve its representative capability, the 1996 IGC must implement Article 138(3) of the Treaty and introduce a uniform electoral procedure for the Parliament, with effect from

June 1999. This reform would require changes mainly in three countries: the introduction of regional lists in France and Spain, and the introduction of proportional representation in Great Britain. A small supranational list, electing say 25 MEPs, should be added to improve proportionality not only within every member state but across the Union as a whole. Such an innovation might also excite the citizen-elector.

Lastly, the IGC should attach three firmly resolved clauses to the new Treaty by way of instruction to its successor:

- The first would spell out the consequences of further enlargement for the institutions, especially with regard to the Council presidency and its voting system, and the size of the Commission and Parliament.

- The second would make a firm link between accession to the Union and collective security. It would also commit the member states to absorbing WEU within the Union, and to making credible the Union's aspirations to a common defence policy.

- The third would comprise a schedule and timetable for the convening of the new constituent procedure, in conjunction with an agreement to open accession negotiations with the Central European countries.

We hope that the changes outlined here would be sufficient to prevent paralysis and to prepare Europe for making a rapid further advance in building the Union.[46]

NOTES

[1] The main contributor to this Paper was Andrew Duff, Director of the Federal Trust. He wishes to acknowledge the valuable oral and written contributions made towards its completion by other members of the Round Table — both restraint and exhortation.

[2] Article B of the Treaty on European Union.

[3] Articles J.4 and J.10. See p. 16 below.

[4] Article B. See p. 10 below.

[5] Article 189(b). See p. 11 below.

[6] Declaration No. 16 on the hierarchy of Community acts.

[7] Declaration No. 1 on civil protection, energy and tourism.

[8] Declaration No. 8 of the Act of Accession, *Official Journal* C 241/08, 29 August 1994.

[9] The two MEPs are Elmar Brok (EPP) and Elisabeth Guigou (ESP). The group will be chaired by Carlos Westendorp, a Spaniard.

[10] EC *Bulletin*, 6/1994, 1.25.

[11] *Growth, Competitiveness, Employment: the challenges and ways forward into the 21st Century*, EC *Bulletin*, Supplement 6/1993.

[12] See Harry Cowie and John Pinder (eds), *A Recovery Strategy for Europe*, London, Federal Trust, 1993.

[13] For a full discussion of current driving forces and alternative futures, see the report of a Federal Trust study group, *Europe's Future: Four Scenarios*, London, Federal Trust, 1991.

[14] The Treaty on European Union, its origins and consequences, are more fully discussed in Andrew Duff, John Pinder and Roy Pryce (eds), *Maastricht and Beyond: Building the European Union*, London, Routledge for the Federal Trust, 1994.

[15] Article 30(12) of the Single European Act; Article N(2) of the Treaty on European Union.

[16] Articles A and B.

[17] See Duff et al., *Maastricht and Beyond*, op cit.; Richard Corbett, *The Treaty of Maastricht: from conception to ratification — a comprehensive reference guide*, Harlow, Longman, 1993; and *The New Treaty on European Union, Vol. 2: Legal and Practical Analyses*, Brussels, Belmont European Policy Centre, 26 February 1992.

[18] The term 'acquis communautaire' is common EC jargon. It means the body of EC law, policy, principles and practices that has been built up and accepted by the Community institutions and the member states since its foundation in 1951. (A.O. Toth, *The Oxford Encyclopaedia of European Community Law: Vol. 1, International Law,* Oxford, Clarendon Press, 1990, p.9.) The European Commission is regarded as the guardian of the acquis.

[19] Article B.

[20] For a fuller discussion of subsidiarity, see Andrew Duff (ed.), *Subsidiarity within the European Community*, London, Federal Trust, 1993.

[21] Article A.

[22] Article F.

[23] Article 169.

[24] Article 145.

[25] For more discussion on this theme, see the Survey on the European Union in *The Economist*, 22 October 1994.

[26] Margaret Thatcher, *The Downing Street Years*, London, HarperCollins, 1993, p. 761.

[27] These seven countries plus the three Baltic states were mentioned specifically as possible future members by the European Council at Copenhagen in June 1993.

[28] Under Article 10 of the WEU's Treaty of Brussels (1948) member states can withdraw from the organisation after fifty years, i.e. from 1998.

[29] Germany, France, Spain, Belgium and Luxembourg are currently members of the Eurocorps. Other bilateral attempts are being made to construct integrated armed forces, notably between the UK and the Netherlands, and, latterly, between the UK and France.

[30] A European Union with strong federal institutions would have fewer inhibitions about where Europe stops in geographic terms: in any event, by admitting Bulgaria and Romania the EU would be transcending the division of Europe established by the Emperor Diocletian seventeen hundred years ago.

[31] By March 1995 Germany, France, Benelux, Spain and Portugal should have succeeded in creating a single travel zone and joint visa policy. Italy and Greece, although signatories of Schengen, do not yet have the capability to participate.

[32] Article 109j.

[33] *Official Journal* C 348, 31/12/1992.

[34] To date only one Directive, on Works Councils, has been promulgated under the Social Protocol.

[35] See Jacques Santer's speech to the European Parliament on taking office as President of the Commission, 18 January 1995.

[36] Wolfgang Schäuble and Karl Lamers, *Reflections on European Policy*, 1 September 1994. The authors are, respectively, leader and foreign affairs spokesman of the CDU/CSU group in the Bundestag. The paper has been published, together with the speech made by Lamers at a Federal Trust conference in London on 17 November 1994, by the Federal Trust and the Konrad Adenauer Stiftung as *A German Agenda for the European Union*, London, 1994.

[37] See Francesco Capotorti, Meinhard Hilf, Francis G. Jacobs and Jean-Paul Jacqué, *The European Union Treaty: Commentary on the draft adopted by the European Parliament*, Oxford, Clarendon Press, 1986.

[38] See Article B.

[39] Original emphasis. For an earlier account of John Major's European Policy, see his article in *The Economist*, 25 September 1993.

[40] At the Federal Trust conference in November 1994; see note 36 above.

[41] Article 138(3) of the Treaty establishes the need for a uniform electoral procedure of the European Parliament.

[42] See EC *Bulletin*, 3/1994, 1.3.28.

[43] See Balladur's article in *Le Monde*, 30 November 1994. See also the speech by foreign minister Alain Juppé to the Assemblée Nationale on 3 November 1994, in which he said that the EU inner core would have 'enhanced solidarities', and the IGC must not merely be a 'patching-up exercise, but a genuine refounding act for Greater Europe'. Alain Lamassoure speaks of a 'new founders' contract'; and Valéry Giscard d'Estaing of a federal core of 'l'Europe-puissance' and an outer tier of 'l'Europe-espace'.

[44] On 4 November 1992 the government won its 'paving motion' to proceed with ratification by 319 votes to 316; 26 Tory MPs voted against.

[45] See Articles 3 and 3(a).

[46] Detailed proposals for reform of the EU institutions will appear in Federal Trust Paper No. 2, *Building the Union*, to be published in June 1995.